10 STEP DRAWING *People*

Published in 2020 by Search Press Ltd.
Wellwood, North Farm Road
Tunbridge Wells
Kent, TN2 3DR

This book is produced by
The Bright Press, an imprint of the Quarto Group,
The Old Brewery, 6 Blundell Street,
London N7 9BH, United Kingdom
T (0)20 7700 6700
www.QuartoKnows.com

ISBN: 978-1-78221-854-8

Publisher: Mark Searle
Creative Director: James Evans
Managing Editor: Jacqui Sayers
Editor: Abbie Sharman
Design: JC Lanaway

Printed and bound in China

10 STEP DRAWING

People

DRAW 30 PEOPLE IN 10 EASY STEPS

JUSTINE LECOUFFE

Contents

>>> Facial Features & Faces

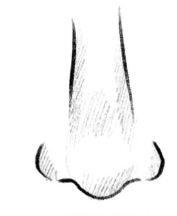

»» Body Parts & Figures

Introduction

In this book, you will find 30 illustrations of people that have been created in just ten simple steps. Whether it's a beautiful portrait of a face or a full figure, it's time to choose your favourite person and get drawing.

Drawing people is easier than you think, because they share the same basic shapes. This book breaks down each facial feature and body part into simple shapes to help you to master them before you use them in a full portrait or figure.

DRAWING FACES

The portraits in this book show the face from multiple angles and explore the shapes of the facial features so you can learn how to change them depending on the position of the face.

Learn how to create each facial feature before putting them together in a ten-step portrait.

DRAWING FIGURES

The book will guide you through the different parts of the body before putting them together into full figures. The step-by-step instructions advise you to use circles or other forms as guides for building the body, and enable you to get the proportions of your people right so you can achieve the overall appearance of different people and bodies.

People come in many shapes and sizes, so don't be afraid to experiment.

COLOURS

Also provided is a colour palette at the end of each finished drawing. Use this as a guide for the different skin tones, but feel free to experiment and use your favourite shades for the hair and clothing.

I hope you will enjoy creating the people in this book as much as I did. Drawing has never been easier!

How to use this book

BASIC EQUIPMENT

Paper: any paper will do, but using sketch paper will give you the best results.

Pencil, eraser and pencil sharpener: try different pencil grades and invest in a good-quality eraser.

Pen: for inking the final image. A medium or fine ink pen is best (ink is better than ballpoint because it dries quickly and is less likely to smudge).

Small ruler: this is optional, but you may find it useful for drawing guidelines.

BLUE AND BLACK LINES

Blue: for your guide shapes. They represent the basic shapes and wireframes of the illustrations. When drawing these shapes, use a pencil so you can rub them out when you're ready.

Black: for the final image. These lines are intended to be part of the final illustration and can be drawn in ink. However, if you're not confident, you can keep these in pencil so you can correct them and then just trace over the final shapes when you have perfected your drawing. Remember to let the ink dry before rubbing out the underlying pencil.

COLOURING

Stay inside the lines and keep your pencils sharp so you have control in the smaller areas.

To achieve a lighter or darker shade, try layering the colour or pressing harder with your pencil.

Hair and clothing can come in many different colours and patterns, so once you're confident with where the shading should be on a figure, why not try varying the colours you use?

You have several options when it comes to colouring your drawings – why not explore them all?

Pencils: this is the simplest option. A good set of coloured pencils with about 24 shades is really all you need.

Paint and paintbrushes: watercolour is probably easiest to work with for beginners, although using acrylic or oil means that you can paint over any mistakes. You'll need two or three brushes of different sizes, with at least one very fine brush.

Facial Features & Faces

Front view
Female eye

This is the traditional eye shape we all know well, and following these simple steps will help you keep the eyes in proportion.

1 Draw a long, curved line that is slightly higher at the outer edge.

2 Create another curved line below this, making the curve more intense. The lines should be slightly parted at the inner corner and connected at the outer corner.

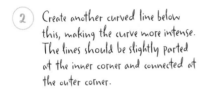

3 Use another curved line above the top line to create the eyelid.

4 Draw the circle of the eye. This consists of the iris (the outer ring) and the pupil (the black middle). The iris should be partly obscured by the eyelid.

5 Draw the eyelashes on the edges of both eyelids. The bottom lash line should have more lashes, but the top line should have longer lashes.

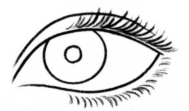

6 Sketch the shape of the eyebrow with pencil. It should begin a bit before the inner corner of the eye and end just beyond the edge of the outer corner.

7 Add a circle and a rectangle to the eye – one on the iris and one on the pupil. This helps to achieve a reflective quality.

8 (a) Fill in the eyebrow using short, curved lines. It should thin out as you advance towards the outer corner.
(b) Colour the pupil and the iris, leaving the previously drawn circles white. Notice that the colour of the iris grows darker while moving upwards, because the eyelid casts a shadow on it.

(a)

(b)

9 If you want to make your eye look like it has makeup applied, colour the top eyelid for an eyeshadow effect, and darken the edges just below the eyelashes for an eyeliner effect.

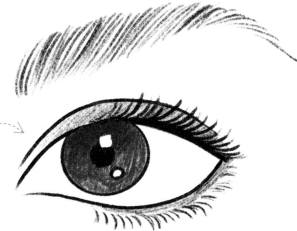

Female nose

The basis of the front view of the nose is a circle and two upward lines, which makes it easy to draw in just five steps.

1. Draw a circle. The size will determine the final size of the nose.

2. Balance two slightly curving vertical lines above the circle.

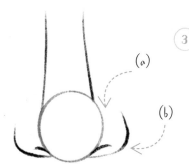

(a)

(b)

3. (a) Add the nostrils by drawing two curved lines from the lower third of the circle, and repeat this on both sides.
(b) Draw the outside of the nostrils by using a curving L-shape and wrapping it slightly around the nostril.

4. To create shading guidelines, draw two vertical lines from the top of the circle (where it meets the bridge of the nose lines) and connect them to the horizontal line two thirds of the way down. When you hit this horizontal line, turn the lines diagonally inwards, so that they follow the curve of the circle back down.

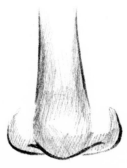

5. Shade along your shading guidelines.

12

Front view
Female ear

The view of the ear is limited from the front, which means that a simple outline shape can be easily achieved.

(1) Start with a simple curved line.

(2) At the top of the first line, add a smaller line underneath.

(3) Continue the second line down and create a small curve just inside the ear.

(4) Create smaller curved lines to add more detail to the ear.

(5) Shade the ear, adding more where the skin folds.

Female mouth

While perfecting your mouth shape, keep the line of the mouth relatively straight. Once you are more confident you can experiment with it to achieve different expressions.

(1) Draw a simple horizontal line for the middle of the lips. Curve the edges slightly to achieve a lightly smiling expression.

14

(2) Using a pencil, sketch two arches to form the outlines for the upper and lower lips.

(3) Use a pen to draw the upper and lower lips following your guides. Make sure to include a dip in the middle of the top lip for the Cupid's bow.

4 Add short arched lines that show the volume of the lips and erase the guides.

5 Shade around the bottom and top lip lines and add some more shadows to the corners of the mouth.

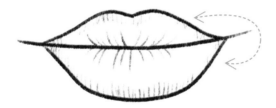

6 Add colour to the lips, adding some darker shades all around the edges. You can choose to have a bold colour or a more natural tone for the lips. If using a natural tone, try choosing a colour a few shades darker than the skin on the face.

Female face 1

Now you've learnt how to draw the different facial features from a front view, try putting them together in this beautiful portrait.

(1) Copy the face shape in pencil and add lines for the neck.

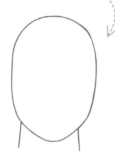

(2) Create guidelines for positioning the eyes, nose and mouth. Add two thin ovals for the eyes.

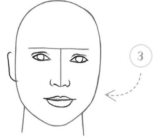

(3) Add detail to the eyes and draw the outline of the mouth. At the end of the nose guidelines, draw the nostrils and edges of the nose. Add the ear.

(4) Draw the outline of the hair. Use the guidelines to place the outlines of the eyebrows.

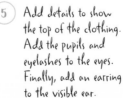

(5) Add details to show the top of the clothing. Add the pupils and eyelashes to the eyes. Finally, add an earring to the visible ear.

6 Refine the face's shape by adjusting the cheeks and chin. Fill in the eyebrows.

7 Erase the guidelines.

8 Keep adding detail to the face and refine the hair.

9 Add shading around the main features to give more detail to the drawing.

10 This drawing has dark, glossy hair and dark red lips.

Female face 2

Try out a bored, moody expression and a loose updo with this female face.
Keep the line of the mouth neutral or slightly down-turned.

1 Draw the face and neck in pencil.

2 Draw guides for the facial features and add the outlines for the eyes.

3 Sketch the eyes, nose and mouth using simple, curving lines. Draw the ears.

4 Draw the outline of the hair, including the parted fringe and escaping hair. Sketch guidelines for the eyebrows.

5 Add detail to the face and ears. Draw the neck of her clothing.

18

6 Use individual strokes to fill in the eyebrows.

7 Rub out any remaining guidelines.

8 Add more detail to the face and include some shading to give shape to the nose and lips.

9 Finish shading the image.

10 Choose the skin tone and hair colour.

Female face 3

Give this next woman a rounder face, a soft expression and long, wavy, dark hair. Keep the colouring soft for a natural look.

(1) Use an oval shape for the face and two lines for the neck.

(2) Draw guidelines on the face and add two slightly slanting eye shapes.

(3) Add the iris and eyelids. Use the nose guide to draw the nostrils and edges of the nose.

20

(4) Use slightly wavy lines to create the outline of the hair. Draw the outlines for the eyebrows.

(5) Fill in the eye detail and add the neckline.

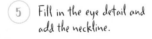

6 Refine the face's shape by adjusting the cheeks and chin. Then fill in the eyebrows.

7 Remove the guidelines.

8 Keep adding detail and refine the hair outline.

9 Add shading around the main features and under the chin.

10 Add colour.

Front view
Female face 4

Follow these simple steps to create a portrait and tackle an Afro.
Try out different hairstyles and textures to create something unique.

1. Copy this face shape using a pencil.

2. Create guidelines for the eyes, nose and mouth. Use two thin ovals for the eyes.

3. Draw the outline shapes of the eyes, mouth and nose.

4. Using tight curves, draw the outline of the hair, shaping it around the head. Use a pencil to draw the outlines of the eyebrows.

5. Add detail to the eyes and use four lines to create the straps of the woman's top.

22

6 Adjust the shape of the cheeks and chin to refine the face's shape. Fill in the eyebrows.

7 Rub out the guides.

8 Add more detail and depth to the eyes and eyebrows.

23

9 Add most of the shading on the hair around the face.

10 Use a darker skin tone and a complementary hair colour.

Front view
Male eye

Draw a male eye in just nine easy steps. The larger eyebrow has less of
an arch than the female version and the eyelashes are less controlled.

1 Draw a long, slightly curved line.

2 Create a more intense curved line below your original line. Connect the lines at the outer corner but leave them slightly parted for the inner corner.

3 The eyelid is another curved line above the eye shape.

4 Draw the circle of the eye, including the iris (the outer ring) and the pupil (the black middle). The iris should be partly obscured by the eyelid.

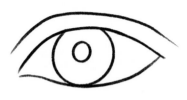

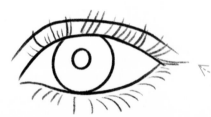

5 Draw the eyelashes on the edges of both eyelids. The top and bottom lashes should be similar in a male eye.

6 Use a pencil to draw the eyebrow shape. It should be gently sloped and begin just before the inner corner of the eye and end just beyond the outer corner.

7 Add a small circle and rectangle on the iris, placing one either side of the pupil.

(a)

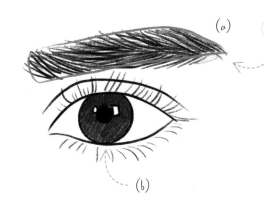

(b)

8 (a) Fill in the eyebrow using short lines. Place some hairs below the outer corner for a natural look. (b) Colour the pupil and the iris leaving white reflections. The colour of the iris should grow darker while moving upwards, because of the shadow of the eyelid.

9 Rub out any remaining guide shape around the eyebrow.

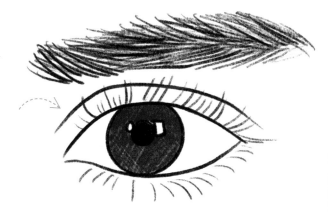

Male nose

Use a circle and two vertical lines to create a simple nose shape.
Make the nose look more masculine by making it wider.

① Draw a circle. The size will determine the final size of the nose, so it should be slightly larger than the average female nose.

② Place two vertical lines above the circle.

③ Use a curving L-shape to form the outside of the nostril. Trace around the bottom of the circle and create a small curve at each side to form the bottom of the nose.

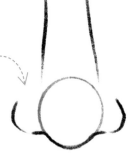

④ Draw two vertical lines from the top of the circle (where it meets the bridge of the nose lines) and connect them to the horizontal line two thirds of the way down. When you hit this horizontal line, turn the lines diagonally inward so that they follow the curve of the circle back down.

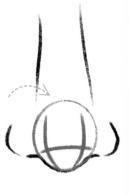

⑤ Shade along the guides but avoid making the circle of the nose too button-like, as this gives a more feminine quality.

26

Front view
Male ear

Men tend to have shorter hair, so their ears are often more visible;
but from this viewpoint, the shape of the ear is simple.

1. Start with a simple curved line.

2. At the top of the first line, add a smaller line underneath.

3. Continue the second line down and create a small curve just inside the ear.

4. Create smaller curved lines to add more detail to the ear.

5. Shade the ear, adding more where the skin folds.

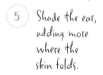

Male mouth

Keep the line of the mouth relatively straight to achieve a neutral expression. The shape of the lips can differ across the sexes and in different racial groups, so look closely at your subject.

1   Draw a slightly wavy line for the middle of the lips.

28

2   Sketch two arches to form the outlines for the upper and lower lips.

3   Use curving lines to draw the upper and lower lips. Make sure to include a dip in the middle of the top lip for the Cupid's bow, but it can be less pronounced than in the female version.

4 Add short arched lines to give the impression of creases in the lips.

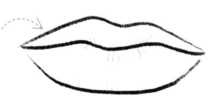

5 Shade around the bottom and top lip lines and add some more shadows to the corners of the mouth.

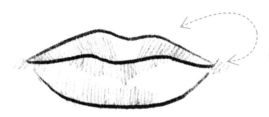

6 Use a skin tone to add some colour to the lips. Add some darker shades all around the edges.

Male face 1

Now you've learnt how to draw the different male facial features from a front view, try putting them together.

1. Copy the face shape in pencil and add lines for the neck.

2. Create guidelines for the facial features. Add two thin ovals for the eyes.

3. Add detail to the eyes, nose and mouth. Try sketching light marks from the corners of the eyes to line up the outer edges of the nostrils.

4. Draw the ears, lining them up just below the eyes. Sketch the outline of the hair and the eyebrows.

5. Add detail to the inner ear.

6 Refine the face's shape by adjusting the cheeks and chin.

7 Using short strokes, fill in the eyebrows. Draw the neckline of his top.

8 Rub out the guides.

9 Add shading around the facial features and under the chin.

10 Use an orange for the hair and facial hair.

Front view

Male face 2

Excited to try out some more facial hair? Follow these steps to draw a man with a tamed beard and moustache.

1 Use an oval and two lines for the face and neck.

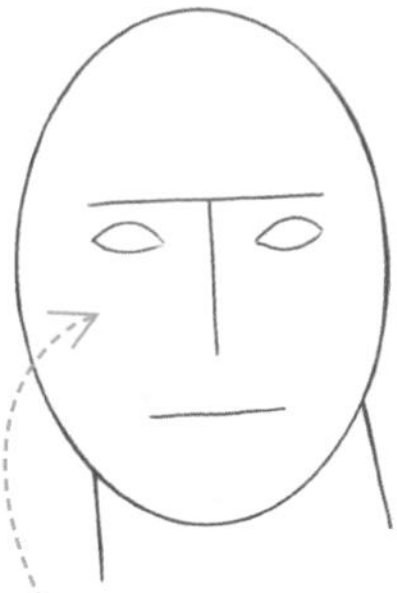

2 Draw straight lines to add facial feature guides. Add ovals for the eyes.

3 Add eyelids and irises to the eyes. Draw the outline of the nose and mouth.

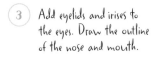

4 Sketch the outline of the hair and moustache. Add the ears. Use pencil to draw the outline of the eyebrows.

5 Refine the face shape with a beard.

6 Sketch eyelashes on the top and bottom lash lines. Add marks at the bridge of the nose to add shape.

7 Draw the eyebrows with short strokes. Add shoulders and create a V-shaped neck for the man's T-shirt. Remove the guidelines.

8 Add more detail to the hair and beard.

9 Shade the inner ear and around the nose and eyes.

10 Use a bright colour for the top, with a darker shade of the same colour for the neck. Use short curved strokes for the hair.

Male face 3

Try using a rounder face and a modern haircut to create a young adult or teenager. Don't include any indication of stubble for a better result.

1   Use a rough oval shape for the face and two lines for the neck.

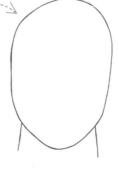

2   Draw guidelines on the face and add two narrow eye shapes.

3   Sketch the basic shapes for the eyes, mouth and nose.

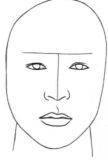

34

4   Use curving strokes to create the outline of the hair. Add the ears and eyebrow shape.

5   Draw the eyebrows.

6 Refine the face and neck. Use a curve for the neckline of his top.

7 Remove any remaining guidelines.

8 Add more detail to the eyebrows, hair and inner ear.

9 Shade more on one side of the face and in areas also in darkness.

10 Add colour.

Male face 4

Follow these simple steps to create a male portrait with longer hair and glasses. Make the mouth slightly upturned to give him a friendly expression.

1 Copy the face shape in pencil and add lines for the neck.

2 Create guidelines for the eyes, nose and mouth. Add two thin ovals for the eyes.

3 Add detail to the eyes and mouth. At the end of the nose guidelines, draw the nostrils and edges of the nose.

4 Using long, flowing lines, draw the outline of the hair. Sketch in some guides for the eyebrows.

5 Add details to show the top of the clothing and fill in the eyebrows.

6 Refine the face's shape by adjusting the cheeks and chin. Remove the guides.

7 Imagine where the ears would be, to help you position the glasses over the eyes.

8 Sketch more detail into the hair and eyebrows.

9 Add more texture to the hair with long strokes and add shading.

10 Colour in the image using the palette here or by picking your own.

Female eye

The eye has a very different shape from the side, but once you
know the differences you'll be able to draw it easily.

(1) Draw a triangle shape
with a slightly curved
front edge.

(2) Add the eyelid on
top of the shape.

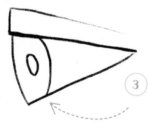

(3) Draw the iris and
a circle within it, which
will become the pupil.

(4) Fill in the pupil with a black
pencil or pen and draw a circular
shape next to it, which will
represent the light reflection.

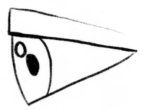

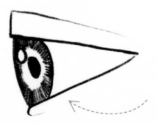

(5) Add tint to the iris
of the eye.

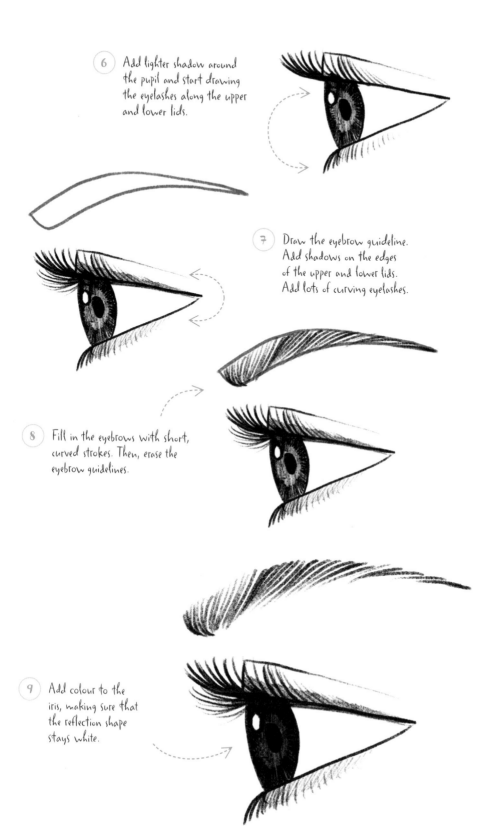

6 Add lighter shadow around the pupil and start drawing the eyelashes along the upper and lower lids.

7 Draw the eyebrow guideline. Add shadows on the edges of the upper and lower lids. Add lots of curving eyelashes.

8 Fill in the eyebrows with short, curved strokes. Then, erase the eyebrow guidelines.

9 Add colour to the iris, making sure that the reflection shape stays white.

Side view
Female nose

A simple nose profile can be created in just five steps. Using circles as a guide will help keep the proportions looking natural.

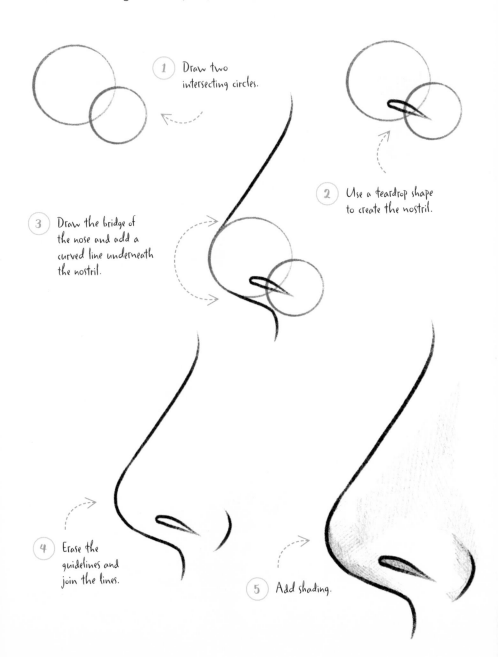

1 Draw two intersecting circles.

2 Use a teardrop shape to create the nostril.

3 Draw the bridge of the nose and add a curved line underneath the nostril.

4 Erase the guidelines and join the lines.

5 Add shading.

Side view
Female ear

Ears can be daunting, but just a few simple curves
can create a realistic shape.

1 Start with
a curved line.

2 Add another curving
shape inside the line.

3 Draw a curved
line for the
inner ear.

4 Add more detail
to the inner ear.

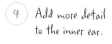
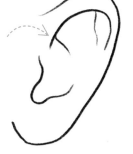

5 Add jewellery to
the earlobe.

6 Shade the ear, paying
particular attention
to the inside.

Female mouth

The side view of lips can be created by starting with a simple triangle. Give the lips a natural feel with smooth but not completely straight lines.

① Draw a triangle and divide it down the middle with a straight line.

② Sketch the mouth's corner.

③ Create a curve that starts at the top left corner of the triangle.

④ Connect the curve you just drew to the corner of the mouth. It's better to draw a slightly curved line than a completely straight one.

⑤ To draw the bottom lip, start your stroke from the bottom left corner of the triangle and follow it through until it touches the top lip.

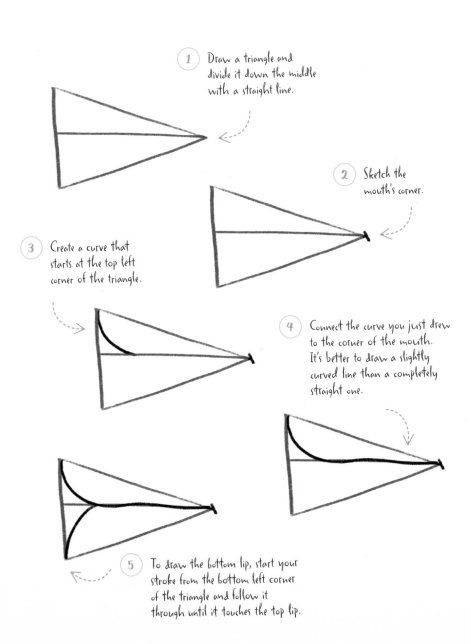

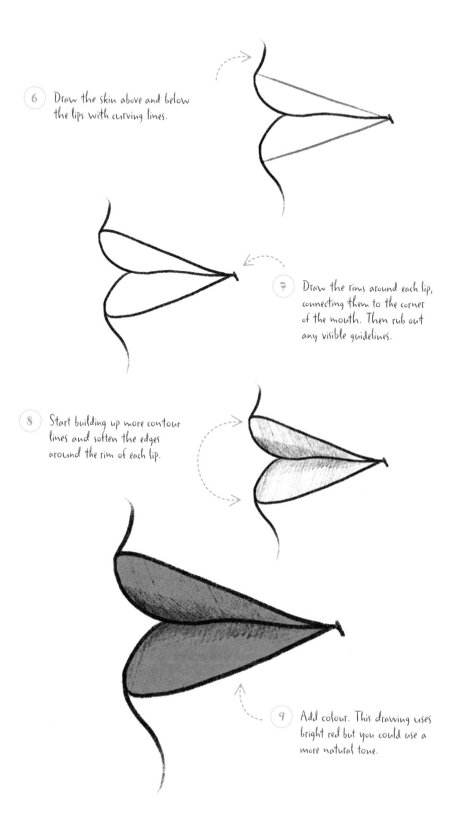

6 Draw the skin above and below the lips with curving lines.

7 Draw the rims around each lip, connecting them to the corner of the mouth. Then rub out any visible guidelines.

43

8 Start building up more contour lines and soften the edges around the rim of each lip.

9 Add colour. This drawing uses bright red but you could use a more natural tone.

Female face 1

Now you've learnt how to draw the different facial features as they appear
from the side, try putting them together in this simple portrait.

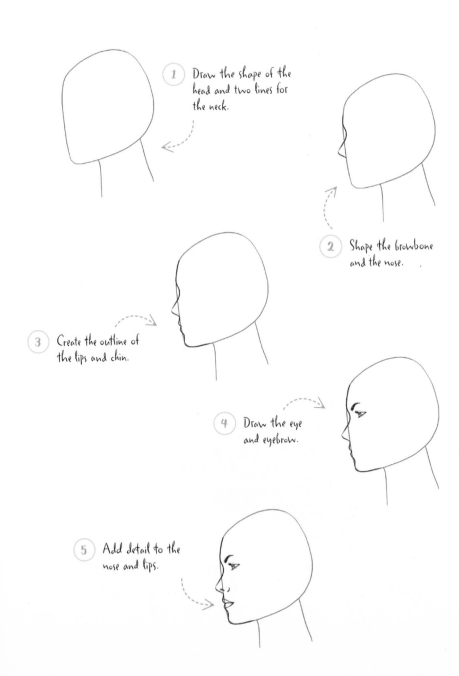

1 Draw the shape of the
head and two lines for
the neck.

2 Shape the browbone
and the nose.

3 Create the outline of
the lips and chin.

4 Draw the eye
and eyebrow.

5 Add detail to the
nose and lips.

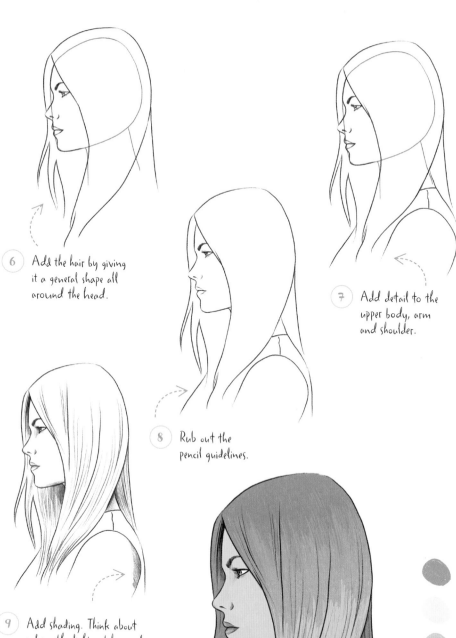

6 Add the hair by giving it a general shape all around the head.

7 Add detail to the upper body, arm and shoulder.

8 Rub out the pencil guidelines.

9 Add shading. Think about where the light catches and where the shadow falls.

10 Use a neutral colour for the top and a light skin tone for the skin. Use multiple shades of brown for the hair, thinking about where the light hits it.

Female face 2

When women wear their hair up and are drawn from the side, it gives a
perfect view of the ear. This portrait will help you to practise the ear shape.

1. Draw a simple face
   shape in pencil and
   add the neck.

2. Create guidelines for the
   eye, eyebrow and mouth.
   Add a triangular shape for
   the eye. Starting from the
   eyebrow line, draw the
   outline of the nose.

46

3. Draw the outline of the
   lips and the forehead.

4. Add detail to the
   eye and eyebrow
   along the guidelines.

5. Draw the lips
   and nostrils.

6 Roughly sketch the outline of the hair and the ear.

7 Draw the collar of the girl's jacket.

8 Rub out the guidelines and add more detail to the face, ear and hair.

9 Add shading around the main features, towards the bottom of the hair and below the bun.

10 Use a skin tone for the face and neck and a dark colour for the hair.

Female face 3

Try pulling the hair to one side and showing it appearing from behind
the head, to show long hair without obscuring the face.

1. Copy the face shape in
pencil and add lines
for the neck.

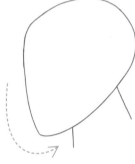

2. Use guides for the facial
features. From the eyebrow
guide, draw the shape of
the nose.

3. Draw the outline
of the lips and
the forehead.

48

4. Give the eye an iris, pupil
and eyelashes, and cover it
with an arching brow.

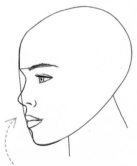

5. Use curved lines to add
the nostril and lips.

6 Slightly above the line of the head, draw the outline of the hair. Add the ear.

7 Draw the clothing around the neck.

8 Rub out the guidelines and add more detail to the hair.

9 Add any shading. This will be limited on this portrait because the light is direct.

10 Add colour.

49

Side view
Male eye

The male eye from the side is similar to the female version except it has a heavier lid, fewer lashes and a thicker eyebrow above it.

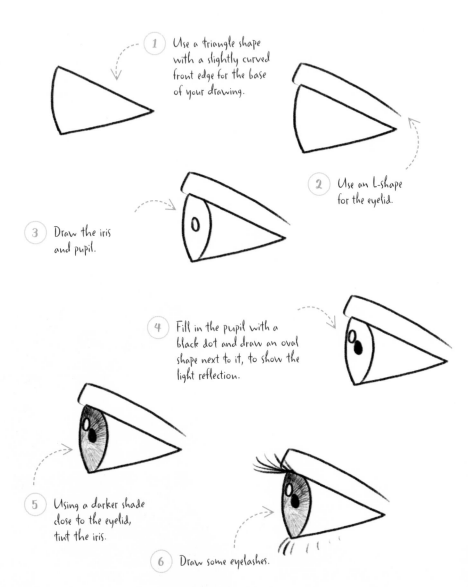

1. Use a triangle shape with a slightly curved front edge for the base of your drawing.

2. Use an L-shape for the eyelid.

3. Draw the iris and pupil.

4. Fill in the pupil with a black dot and draw an oval shape next to it, to show the light reflection.

5. Using a darker shade close to the eyelid, tint the iris.

6. Draw some eyelashes.

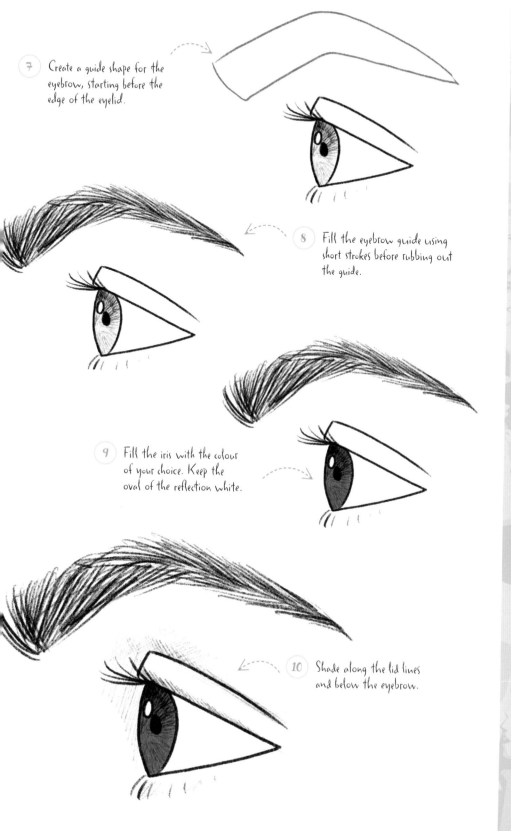

7　Create a guide shape for the eyebrow, starting before the edge of the eyelid.

8　Fill the eyebrow guide using short strokes before rubbing out the guide.

51

9　Fill the iris with the colour of your choice. Keep the oval of the reflection white.

10　Shade along the lid lines and below the eyebrow.

Side view
Male nose

Follow these five simple steps to transform two circles into a natural male nose.

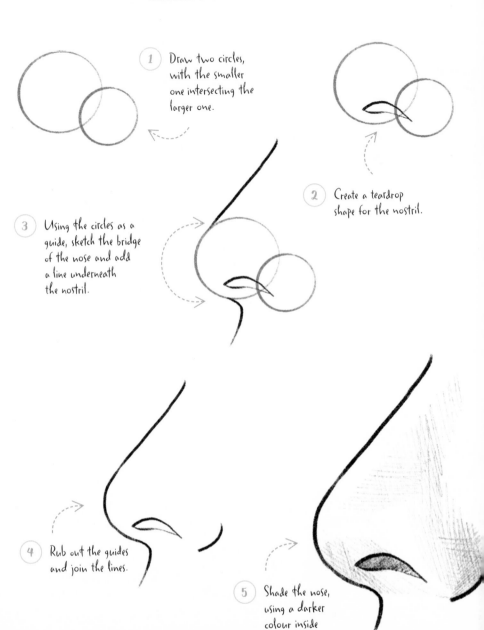

1. Draw two circles, with the smaller one intersecting the larger one.

2. Create a teardrop shape for the nostril.

3. Using the circles as a guide, sketch the bridge of the nose and add a line underneath the nostril.

4. Rub out the guides and join the lines.

5. Shade the nose, using a darker colour inside the nostril.

Side view
Male ear

Ears don't need to be daunting – follow these five simple steps
to create a realistic shape for your drawing.

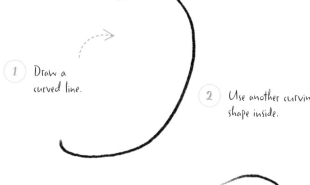

1 Draw a
   curved line.

2 Use another curving
   shape inside.

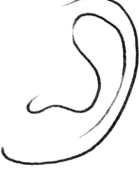

3 Following the first curve,
   create the inner edge of
   the ear.

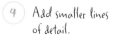

4 Add smaller lines
   of detail.

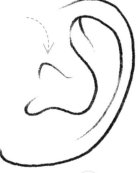

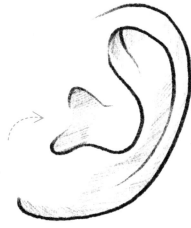

5 Shade the ear, paying
   particular attention
   to the inside.

Side view
Male mouth

Use a simple triangle as the base shape for creating a side view of the lips.
These steps and results will be very similar to a side view of female lips.

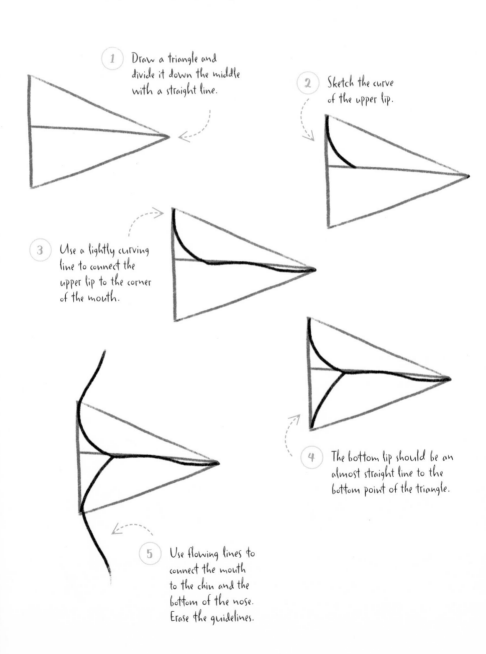

1 Draw a triangle and divide it down the middle with a straight line.

2 Sketch the curve of the upper lip.

3 Use a lightly curving line to connect the upper lip to the corner of the mouth.

4 The bottom lip should be an almost straight line to the bottom point of the triangle.

5 Use flowing lines to connect the mouth to the chin and the bottom of the nose. Erase the guidelines.

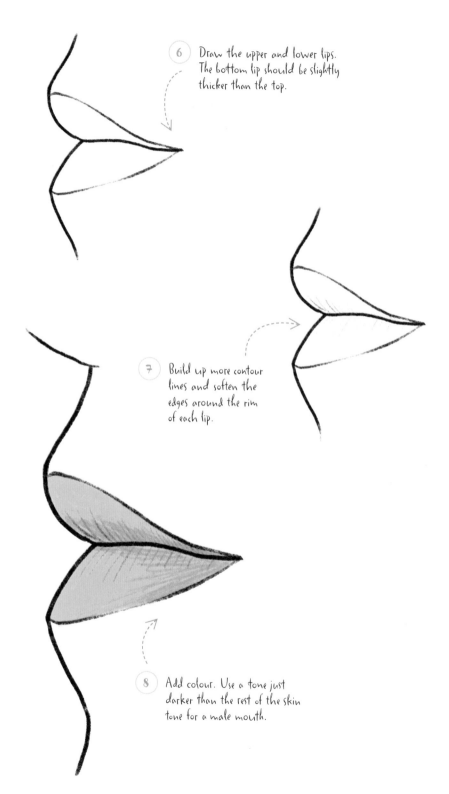

6 Draw the upper and lower lips. The bottom lip should be slightly thicker than the top.

7 Build up more contour lines and soften the edges around the rim of each lip.

8 Add colour. Use a tone just darker than the rest of the skin tone for a male mouth.

Side view
Male face 1

Now you've learnt the how to draw the different male facial features from a side view, try putting them together. Have fun drawing the Afro!

1. Draw a rough face shape in pencil and add the neck.

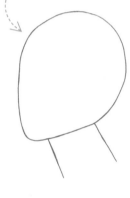

2. Add guidelines for the eyebrow and mouth. Use a triangular shape for the eye.

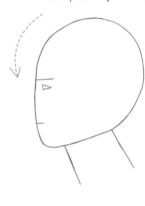

3. Draw the outline of the nose.

4. Draw the outline of the lips and extend the nose into the forehead.

5. Create a guide for the eyebrow and add detail to the eye. Use tightly curving lines to draw the outline of the hair.

6 Fill in the eyebrow and draw some facial hair above the top lip. Add the nostril.

7 Rub out the guidelines.

8 Refine the hair and draw the neck area. Add a zipped jacket.

9 Add shading around the main features to give more detail to the drawing.

10 Add colour.

Side view
Male face 2

This drawing will give you the opportunity to work on your facial hair drawing skills, with a full but well-groomed beard from a side view.

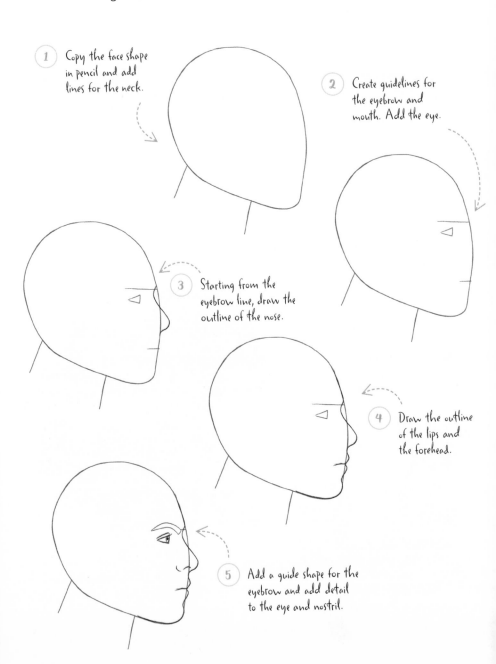

1 Copy the face shape in pencil and add lines for the neck.

2 Create guidelines for the eyebrow and mouth. Add the eye.

3 Starting from the eyebrow line, draw the outline of the nose.

4 Draw the outline of the lips and the forehead.

5 Add a guide shape for the eyebrow and add detail to the eye and nostril.

6 Draw the outline of the hair and the ear.

7 Fill in the eyebrow.

8 Refine the hair and draw the high neck of the man's coat. Then, rub out the guidelines.

9 Add shading around the main features and the edges of the hair.

10 Use colour to add more detail.

Side view
Male face 3

Attempting to draw glasses from a side view can seem daunting, but these ten simple steps will help you create this cool character!

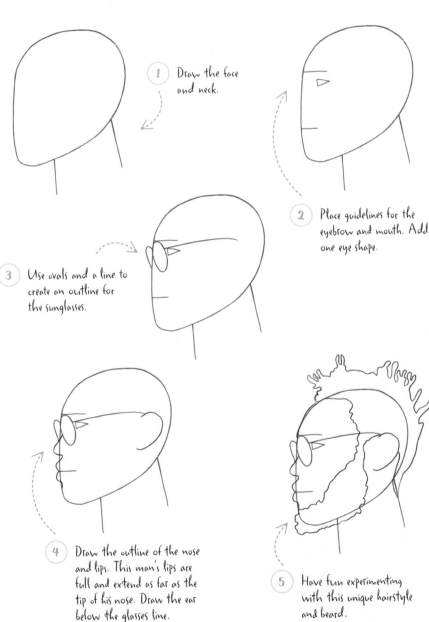

1. Draw the face and neck.

2. Place guidelines for the eyebrow and mouth. Add one eye shape.

3. Use ovals and a line to create an outline for the sunglasses.

4. Draw the outline of the nose and lips. This man's lips are full and extend as far as the tip of his nose. Draw the ear below the glasses line.

5. Have fun experimenting with this unique hairstyle and beard.

6. Add detail to the eye and create the moustache.

7. Draw the frames of the sunglasses and rub out the guide shapes.

8. Sketch in the eyebrow and draw the clothing.

9. Add shading around the main features to give more detail to the drawing.

10. Give the man a darker skin tone and use black for his hair.

Three-quarter view
Female eye

This view is similar to a front view but has some small and important differences. Follow these simple steps to make sure your version is perfect.

1 Draw two curved lines.

2 Add a line above this to create the upper eyelid. You can also add a smaller line below the eye to show the lower lid, but this should be subtle.

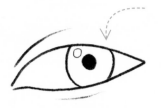

3 Draw a circle to represent the iris and a small circle within it for the pupil. Add a circle next to the pupil to show the reflection of light in the eye.

4 Sketch in some shading for the iris. Keep it lighter around the pupil.

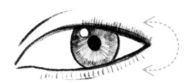

5 Shade around the upper and lower lid. Starting at the middle and working towards the outer corner of the eye, start to add the eyelashes.

6 Draw the shape of the eyebrow in pencil.

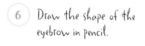

7 Fill in the shape of the eyebrow with short curving lines for the hairs. Erase the pencil guide.

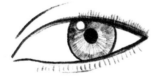

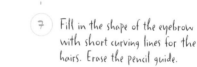

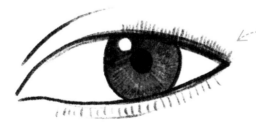

8 Colour the iris of the eye, leaving the light-reflection circle empty.

Female nose

A 3D triangle and two circles are all it takes to give shape to this nose.

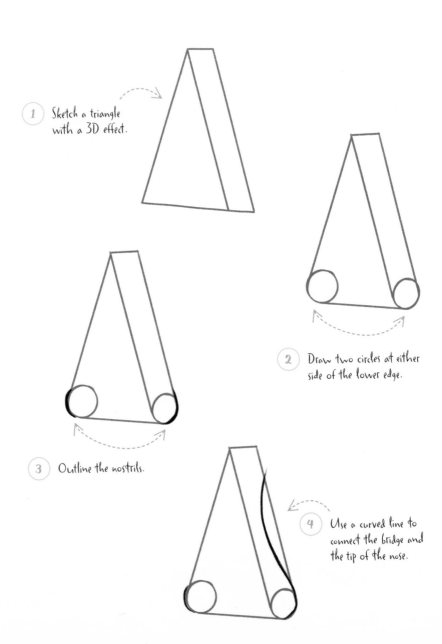

1. Sketch a triangle with a 3D effect.

2. Draw two circles at either side of the lower edge.

3. Outline the nostrils.

4. Use a curved line to connect the bridge and the tip of the nose.

64

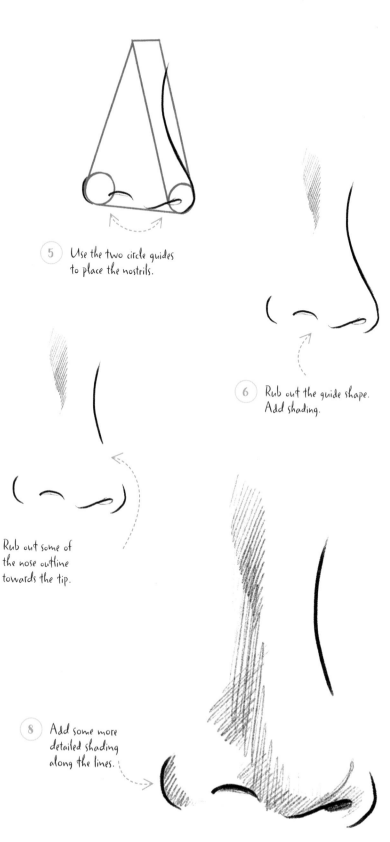

5 Use the two circle guides to place the nostrils.

6 Rub out the guide shape. Add shading.

7 Rub out some of the nose outline towards the tip.

8 Add some more detailed shading along the lines.

Three-quarter view
Female mouth

The key to a perfectly proportioned mouth from this view is to use the vertical and horizontal guides to help with the positioning of the middle of the lips.

1. Draw two intersecting lines. The vertical line should be placed three quarters of the way along the horizontal guide from the right.

2. Trace the line between the lips along the horizontal guide.

3. Create the lines for the upper and lower lips. The vertical guide should touch the middle dip of the top lip and the fullest part of the bottom lip.

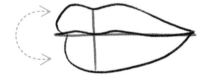

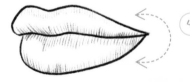

4. Start adding some shading to the lips, along the lip lines.

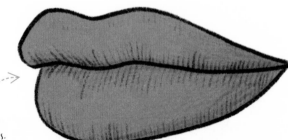

5. Add colour to the lips, using darker shades close to the lines.

Female ear

This ear is a cross between the simple front-on view of the ear and a side-on view. Keep the ear relatively close to the head and add more detail inside.

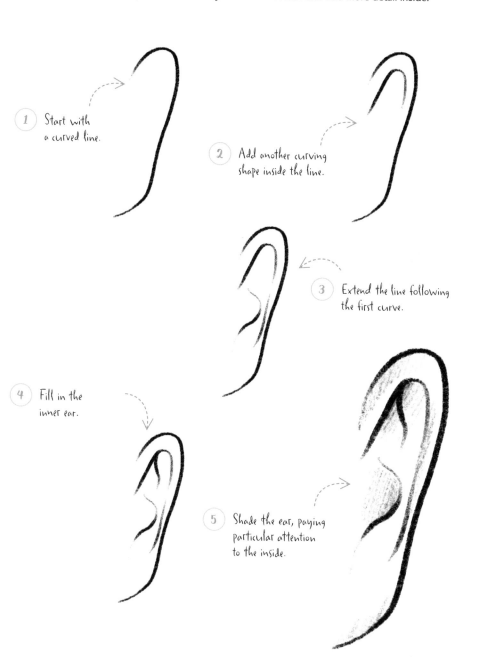

1. Start with a curved line.

2. Add another curving shape inside the line.

3. Extend the line following the first curve.

4. Fill in the inner ear.

5. Shade the ear, paying particular attention to the inside.

67

Three-quarter view
Female face 1

Now you have a grasp of the different elements,
try putting them together in this cute portrait.

1. Copy the face shape in pencil and add lines for the neck.

2. Create guidelines for the eyes, nose and mouth. Add two thin ovals for the eyes.

3. Add detail to the eyes, nose and mouth.

4. Draw the outline of the hair and create a guide for the eyebrows.

5. Give the eyes more detail. Add the outline of her clothing.

6 Refine the face's shape by adjusting the cheeks and chin. Fill in the eyebrows.

7 Rub out the guidelines.

8 Keep adding detail, then refine the hair outline.

9 Add shading around the main features to give more detail to the drawing.

10 Add colour.

Three-quarter view
Female face 2

Give your portrait some added personality with decorative elements.
This woman has a flower behind her ear, which gives her an exotic quality.

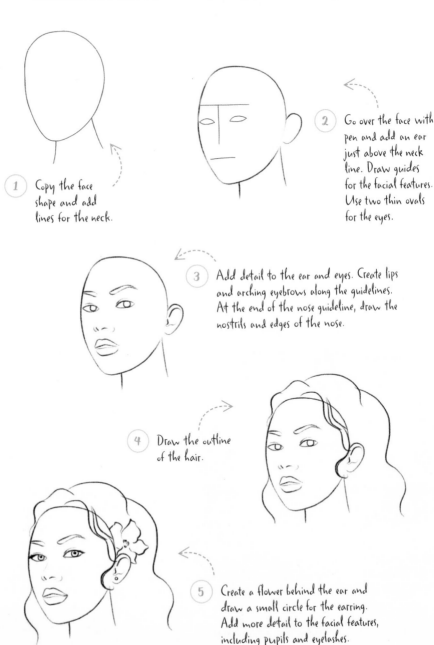

1 Copy the face shape and add lines for the neck.

2 Go over the face with pen and add an ear just above the neck line. Draw guides for the facial features. Use two thin ovals for the eyes.

3 Add detail to the ear and eyes. Create lips and arching eyebrows along the guidelines. At the end of the nose guideline, draw the nostrils and edges of the nose.

4 Draw the outline of the hair.

5 Create a flower behind the ear and draw a small circle for the earring. Add more detail to the facial features, including pupils and eyelashes.

(6) Fill in the main dark shades.

(7) Use shading to add more detail to the image, particularly on the lips, around the nose and in the ear.

(8) Add more shape to the face, paying close attention to the cheek and the jawline on the right. Add more detail to the flower.

(9) Add shading to the face and neck.

(10) Use a skin tone for the face and neck and deeper colours for the lips and flower.

Three-quarter view
Male eye

Consider the small differences between this view of the eye and
a front view, then keep to these steps to master this drawing.

(1) Draw two curved lines.

(2) Add a line above this to create the
upper eyelid. You can also add a
smaller line below the eye to show the
lower lid, but this should be subtle.

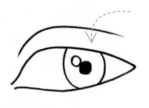

(3) Draw a circle to represent the iris and
a small circle within it for the pupil.
Add a circle next to the pupil to show
the reflection of light in the eye.

(4) Sketch in some shading for the iris.
Keep it lighter around the pupil.

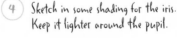

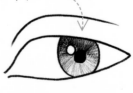

5 Shade around the upper and lower lid. Starting at the middle and working towards the outer corner of the eye, start to add the eyelashes.

6 Draw the shape of the eyebrow in pencil.

7 Fill in the shape of the eyebrow with short curving lines for the hairs. Erase the pencil guide.

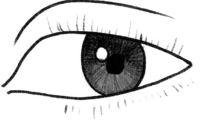

8 Colour the iris of the eye, leaving the light-reflection circle empty.

Three-quarter view
Male nose

A 3D triangle and two circles are all it takes to give shape to this nose.

(1) Draw a triangle with a 3D effect.

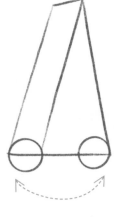

(2) Add two circles at the angles along the lower edge.

(3) Draw the bridge of the nose and create the nose tip.

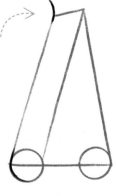

(4) Connect the bridge and the tip with a line. To achieve a natural look, make sure this line is not too straight.

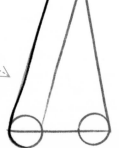

5 Use the second circle guide to trace a line for the back of the nostril.

6 Place the nostril towards the back of the nose.

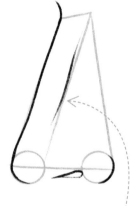

7 Add a parallel line to the other side of the nose.

8 Add some shading along the lines.

Three-quarter view
Male mouth

Use a cross-shaped guide to help with the positioning of the middle of the lips in this slightly off-centre view.

1. Draw two intersecting lines. The vertical line should be placed three quarters of the way along the horizontal guide from the right.

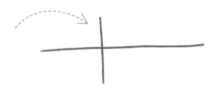

2. Trace the line between the lips along the horizontal guide.

3. Create the lines for the upper and lower lips. The vertical guide should touch the middle dip of the top lip and the fullest part of the bottom lip.

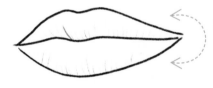

4. Start adding lines to the lips to give them a 3D quality.

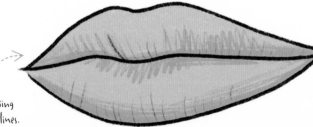

5. Add colour to the lips, using darker shades close to the lines.

Three-quarter view
Male ear

This ear is a cross between the simple front-on view of the ear and a full side-on view. Keep the ear relatively close to the head and add more detail inside.

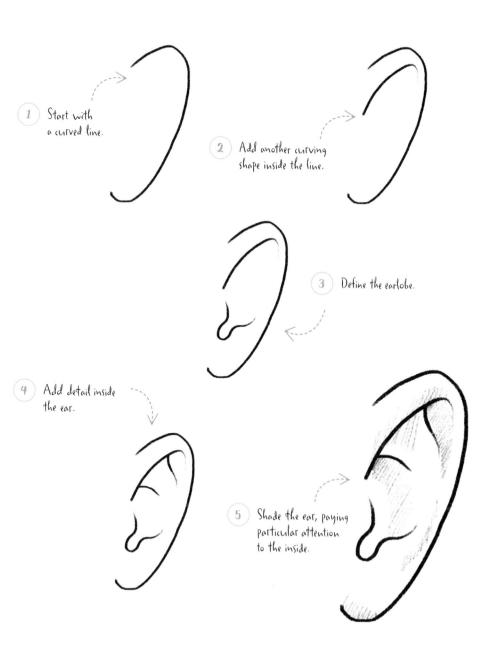

1. Start with a curved line.

2. Add another curving shape inside the line.

3. Define the earlobe.

4. Add detail inside the ear.

5. Shade the ear, paying particular attention to the inside.

Three-quarter view
Male face 1

Now you know the different elements of the male face from a three-quarter view, try putting them together in this cute portrait.

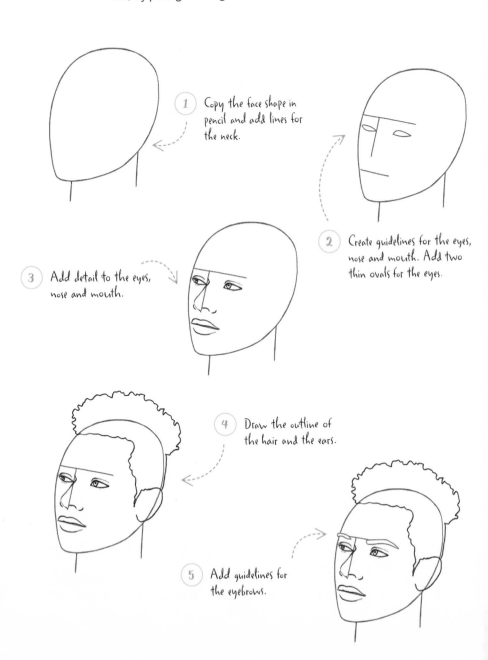

1. Copy the face shape in pencil and add lines for the neck.

2. Create guidelines for the eyes, nose and mouth. Add two thin ovals for the eyes.

3. Add detail to the eyes, nose and mouth.

4. Draw the outline of the hair and the ears.

5. Add guidelines for the eyebrows.

6 Refine the face's shape by adjusting the cheeks and chin. Draw the eyebrows.

7 Rub out the guidelines and add details to the neck, including clothing.

8 Keep adding detail, then refine the hair outline.

9 Add shading around the main features to give more detail to the drawing.

10 Add colour.

Three-quarter view
Male face 2

Add character to your portraits by using different accessories and clothing.
This man has a wide-rimmed hat that gives him an interesting look.

1. Draw the face shape and neck.

2. Place guides for the facial features. Add two thin ovals for the eyes.

3. Add detail to the eyes, nose and mouth.

4. Create the hat and draw the outline of the hair and ear beneath it.

5. Draw the eyebrows.

6 Adjust the cheeks and chin to perfect the face.

7 Remove the guidelines and add the remaining clothing.

8 Add detail to the face, hair and clothing.

9 Shade around the facial features and underneath the back of the hat.

10 Add colour.

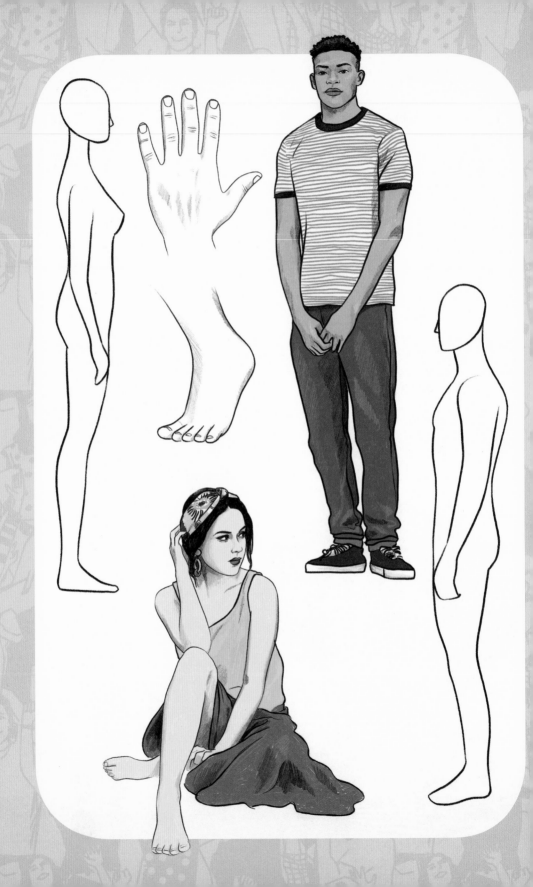

Body Parts
& Figures

Female proportions

The average human body is around eight heads high. The scale below
will help you to understand the proportions of the female body.

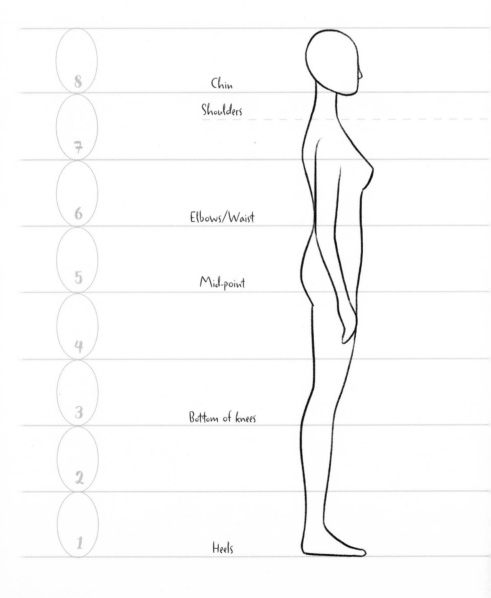

8 — Chin

Shoulders

7

6 — Elbows/Waist

5 — Mid-point

4

3 — Bottom of knees

2

1 — Heels

Wireframe

The wireframe technique is very useful in that it helps you get the main parts of the pose correct and in proportion before adding detail. The wireframe will make drawing the figure an easier task as it will serve as a 'skeleton' for building the rest of the body.

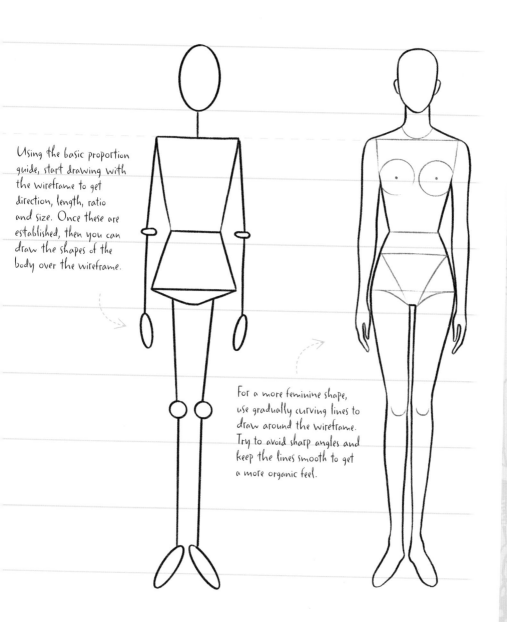

Using the basic proportion guide, start drawing with the wireframe to get direction, length, ratio and size. Once these are established, then you can draw the shapes of the body over the wireframe.

For a more feminine shape, use gradually curving lines to draw around the wireframe. Try to avoid sharp angles and keep the lines smooth to get a more organic feel.

Male proportions

The scale below will help you to understand the proportions of the male body. Again, the average human body is around eight heads high.

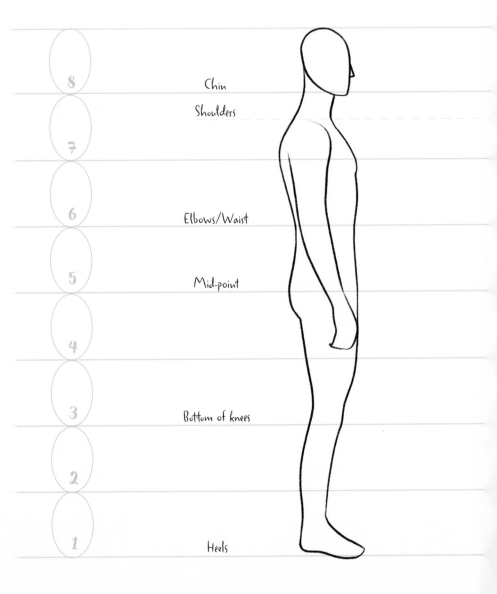

8	Chin
	Shoulders
7	
6	Elbows/Waist
5	Mid-point
4	
3	Bottom of knees
2	
1	Heels

Wireframe

The wireframe technique is very useful in that it helps you get the main parts of the pose correct and in proportion before adding detail. The wireframe will make drawing the figure an easier task as it will serve as a 'skeleton' for building the rest of the body.

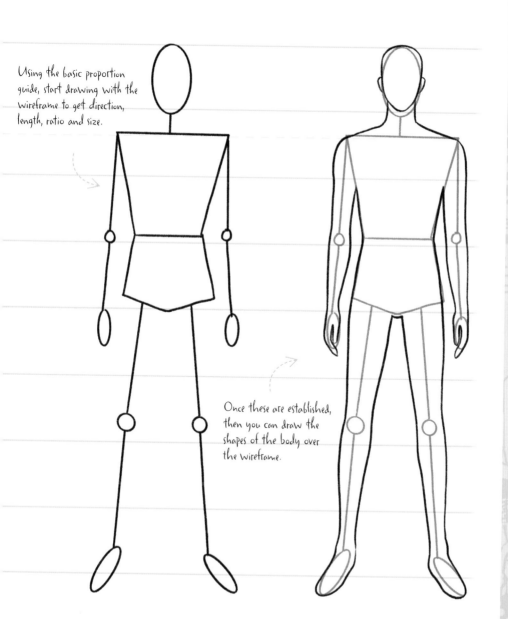

Using the basic proportion guide, start drawing with the wireframe to get direction, length, ratio and size.

Once these are established, then you can draw the shapes of the body over the wireframe.

Hand

The hand is one of the most difficult body parts to draw, but these simple steps will help you to break it down into manageable sections.

1. Draw this shape in pencil lines.

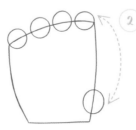

2. Create four circles along the top of the shape and one towards the bottom.

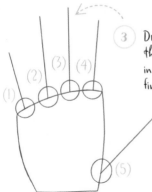

3. Draw five lines, starting from the centre of each circle. Keep in mind that the middle finger is normally the longest.

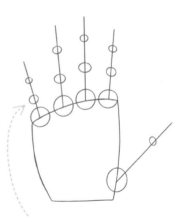

4. Position two more circles along each line, decreasing in size as they get closer to the end of the line. These circles will become the joints of the fingers.

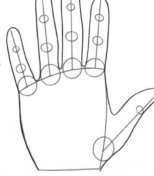

5. Trace the outline of the hand around the guidelines.

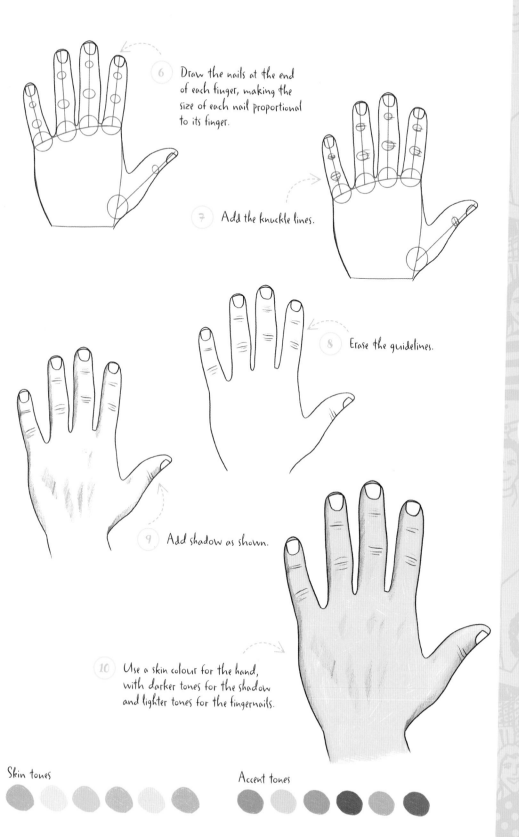

6. Draw the nails at the end of each finger, making the size of each nail proportional to its finger.

7. Add the knuckle lines.

8. Erase the guidelines.

9. Add shadow as shown.

10. Use a skin colour for the hand, with darker tones for the shadow and lighter tones for the fingernails.

Skin tones

Accent tones

Hand positions

Although the basic shape of men's and women's hands are similar, you can give your drawing a more masculine or feminine look by changing the detail.

Female hand examples

Put less emphasis on the joints and knuckles. Keep the fingers long and slender.

Think about feminine poses for the hands. A long fingernail can also give a hand a more feminine look.

Avoid harsh lines and shapes when drawing female hands.

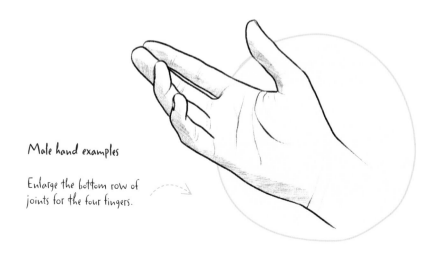

Male hand examples

Enlarge the bottom row of joints for the four fingers.

Accentuate the veins, wrinkles and tendons.

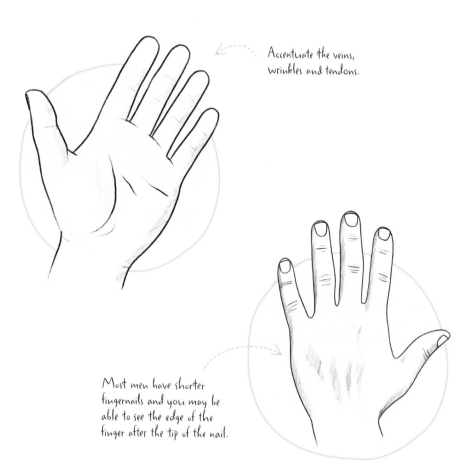

Most men have shorter fingernails and you may be able to see the edge of the finger after the tip of the nail.

Female arm

People come in many shapes and sizes, but a typical female arm is smooth and softly curving. Master these steps and then start experimenting.

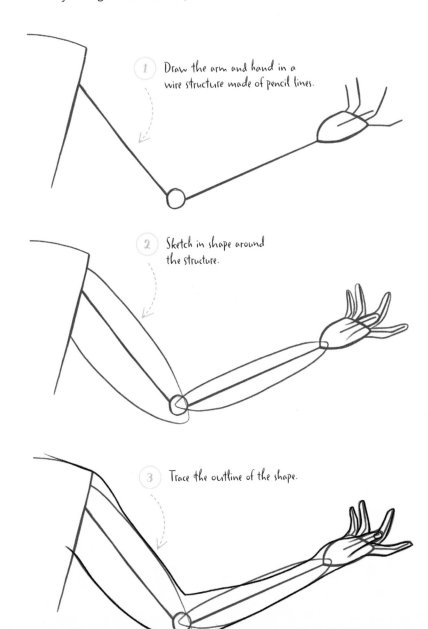

1. Draw the arm and hand in a wire structure made of pencil lines.

2. Sketch in shape around the structure.

3. Trace the outline of the shape.

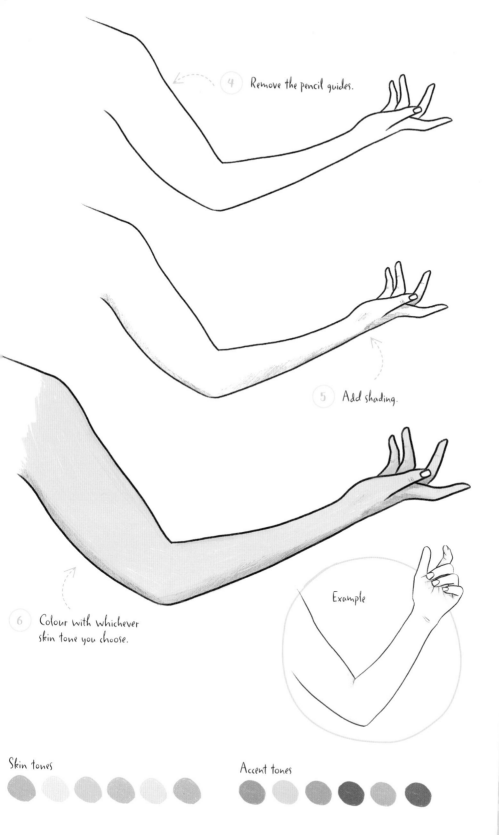

4 Remove the pencil guides.

5 Add shading.

6 Colour with whichever skin tone you choose.

Example

Skin tones

Accent tones

Male arm

A typical male arm is more muscular and defined in shape than a female arm. Remember to accentuate the tendons.

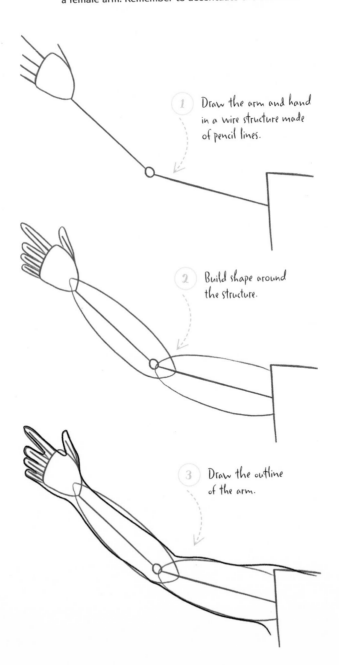

1. Draw the arm and hand in a wire structure made of pencil lines.

2. Build shape around the structure.

3. Draw the outline of the arm.

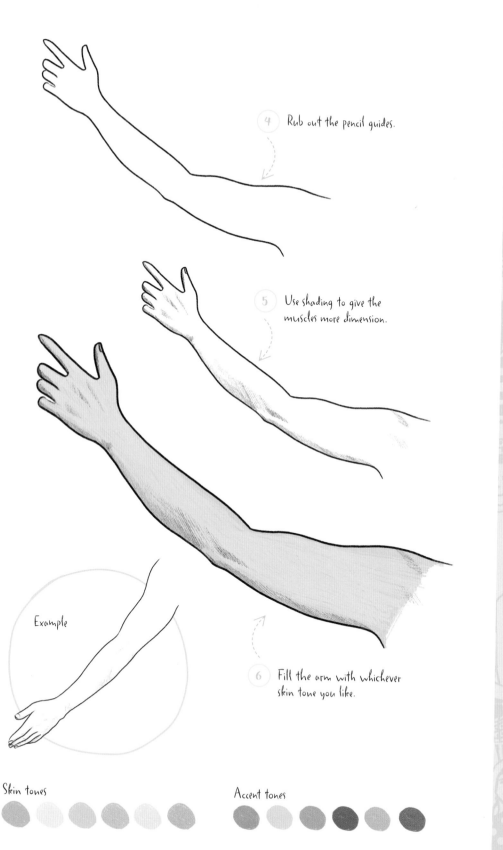

4 Rub out the pencil guides.

5 Use shading to give the
   muscles more dimension.

Example

6 Fill the arm with whichever
   skin tone you like.

95

Skin tones

Accent tones

Foot

Similarly to the hand, the digits on the foot can make it difficult to draw,
but these eight steps will guide you through it.

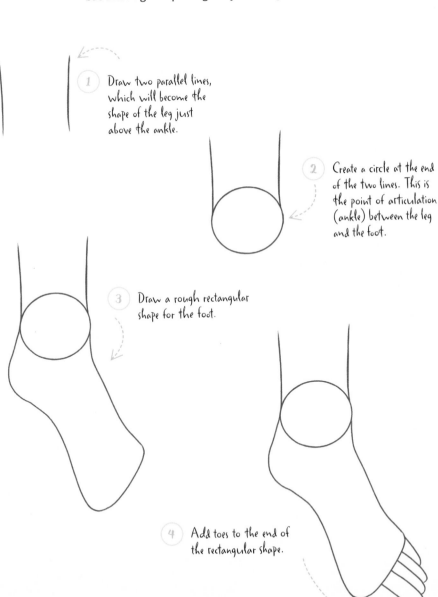

1. Draw two parallel lines, which will become the shape of the leg just above the ankle.

2. Create a circle at the end of the two lines. This is the point of articulation (ankle) between the leg and the foot.

3. Draw a rough rectangular shape for the foot.

4. Add toes to the end of the rectangular shape.

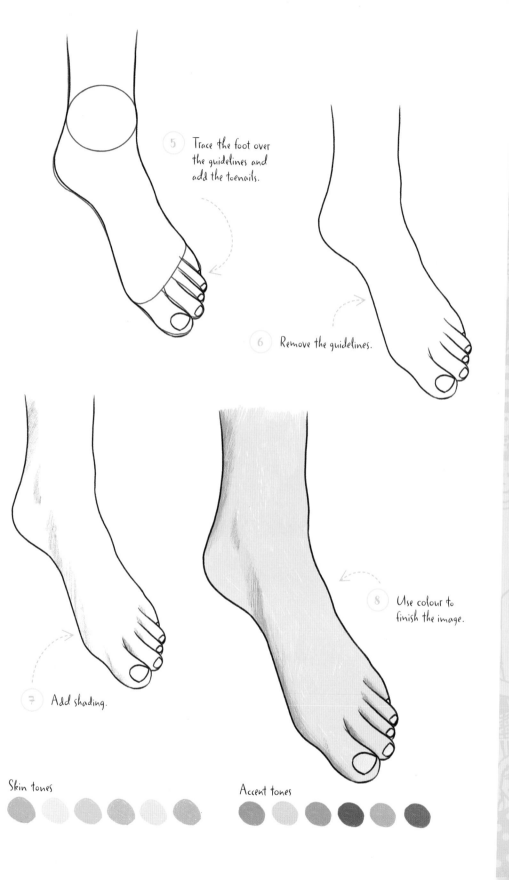

5 Trace the foot over the guidelines and add the toenails.

6 Remove the guidelines.

7 Add shading.

8 Use colour to finish the image.

Skin tones

Accent tones

Foot

Because only a single toe is visible, this view of the foot is easy to master.
Create yours using two lines, a circle and a triangle as a guide.

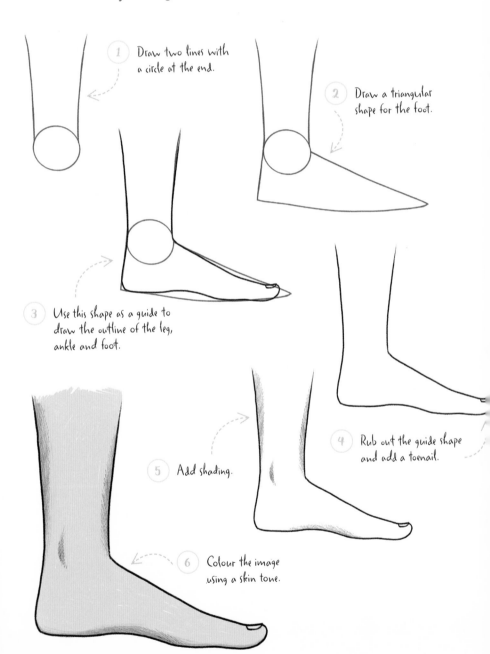

1. Draw two lines with a circle at the end.

2. Draw a triangular shape for the foot.

3. Use this shape as a guide to draw the outline of the leg, ankle and foot.

4. Rub out the guide shape and add a toenail.

5. Add shading.

6. Colour the image using a skin tone.

98

Moving foot

The foot bends and moves as we walk, so try giving your drawings some movement by altering the shape of the foot.

1. Create the ankle using two lines with a circle at the bottom.

2. Draw a rectangle with a triangle at the tip.

3. Use this shape as a guide to draw the outline of the leg, ankle and foot.

4. Rub out the pencil lines.

5. Add toenails and shading.

6. Use colour to finish the image.

Skin tones

Accent tones

Female legs

With these simple steps you can avoid drawing stick legs. Remember that female legs tend to have softer shapes to them than male legs.

1   Draw two vertical lines starting from the upper body shape.

2   Add two circles midline for the knees and two oval shapes for the feet.

3   Sketch additional shape around the lines and circles, roughly tracing the shape of the legs.

4   Trace the final shape over the guidelines and add guides for the toes.

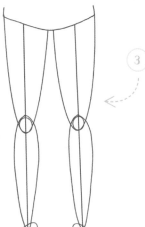
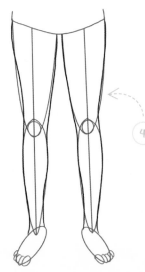

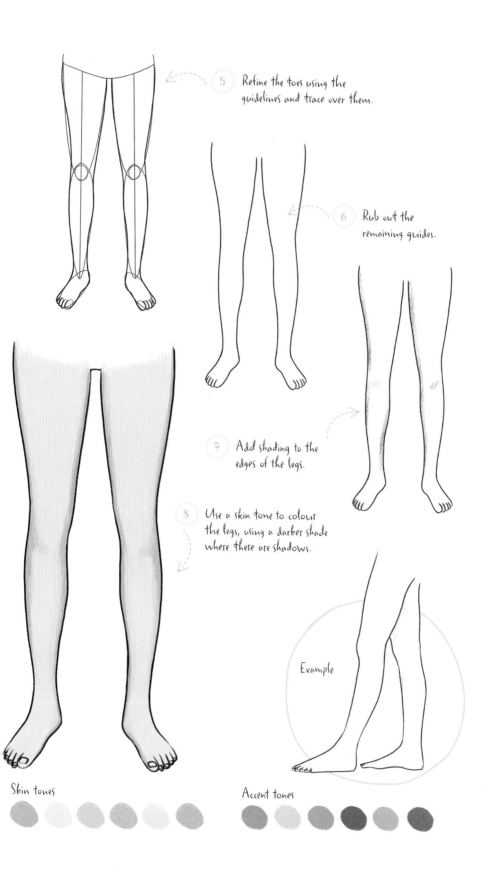

5 Refine the toes using the guidelines and trace over them.

6 Rub out the remaining guides.

7 Add shading to the edges of the legs.

8 Use a skin tone to colour the legs, using a darker shade where there are shadows.

Example

Skin tones

Accent tones

Male legs

Give the legs shape and definition but keep the thighs and lower legs at a similar size, you can play around with the size and proportion once you've mastered these steps.

1. Draw two vertical lines emerging from the upper body shape.

2. Add two circles midline for the knees and two oval shapes for the feet.

3. Give the legs some shape.

4. Use the guidelines to outline the legs, then add guides for the toes.

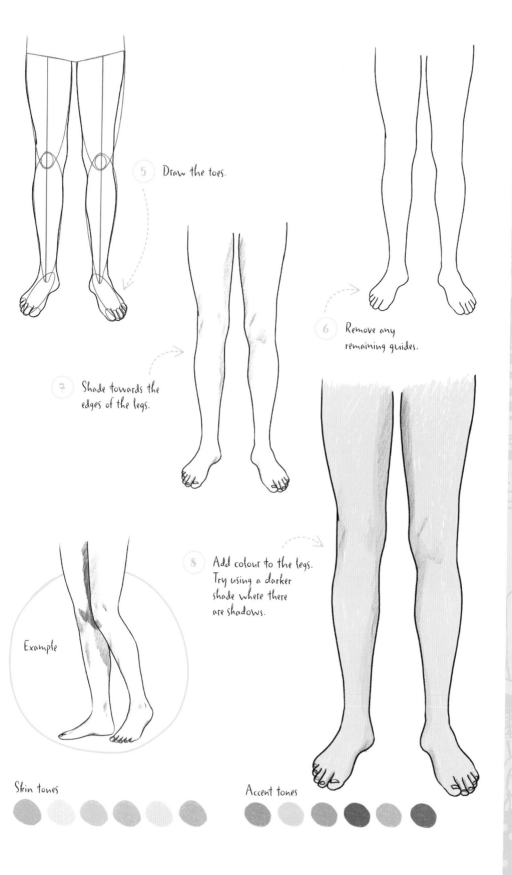

5 Draw the toes.

6 Remove any remaining guides.

7 Shade towards the edges of the legs.

8 Add colour to the legs. Try using a darker shade where there are shadows.

Example

Skin tones

Accent tones

Easy standing woman

This simple standing figure is perfect for your first complete figure.
Add big hair and cool accessories to give your character some personality.

1. Draw a basic body shape and an oval for the head. Connect them with a guideline.

2. Create the limbs using simple shapes around the frame.

3. Give the shoes some detail, develop the hands and add a handbag dangling from the fingertips.

4. Use a soft cloud shape for the hair and connect it to the head with a band.

5. Draw the woman's outfit by using the guides to create a tank top and high-waisted skirt.

6 Using tight curving shapes, add detail to the hair. Draw the facial features.

7 Draw smooth lines along the guide shapes of the limbs. Draw any accessories.

8 Refine the face and add lines for the collarbones and fingernails.

9 Shade the face, body and clothing.

10 Use lighter colours around the edge of the hair and darker colours around the neck. Restrict the clothing colours to blocks.

105

Standing party girl

Take all the aspects you've learnt so far and put them together to draw this girl on her night out. Remember to keep the lines of the legs and arms smooth.

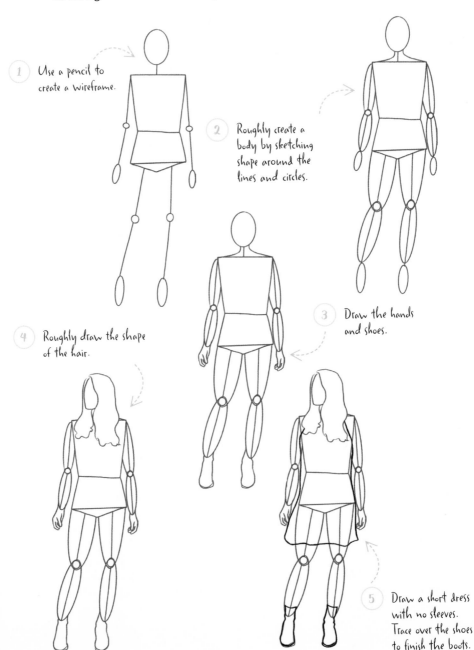

1. Use a pencil to create a wireframe.

2. Roughly create a body by sketching shape around the lines and circles.

3. Draw the hands and shoes.

4. Roughly draw the shape of the hair.

5. Draw a short dress with no sleeves. Trace over the shoes to finish the boots.

6 Sketch around the body, then draw the facial features and add detail to the hair.

7 Add more detail to the face and shoes.

8 Remove the guidelines.

9 Think about the darker areas and add shading, particularly on the legs and arms.

10 Add whichever skin tone you choose to the skin, then use a vivid blue for the dress and a light tone for the hair.

Chic standing woman

You can create this elegant standing pose with just a few tweaks to a classic standing pose. Adusting the pose will give your character a more natural look.

1. Draw a wireframe figure in pencil.

2. Add shape around the lines and circles.

3. Draw the handbag and start adding detail to the hands, feet and shoes.

4. Add the outline of long, sleek hair to the head.

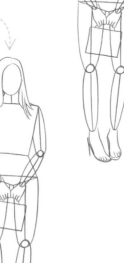

5. Create the woman's long, flowing skirt, bulky jumper and strappy shoes.

6 Draw the facial features and strands of hair.

7 Give the jumper creases and folds. Draw the woman's earring.

8 Rub out the guides and add detail to the face.

9 Add shading to the darker areas.

10 Create a striped pattern on the skirt by leaving lines of white. Add bursts of colour with orange accessories.

Crouching woman

A crouching figure doesn't have to be difficult to draw – focus on getting the position of the wireframe correct and everything else will fall into place.

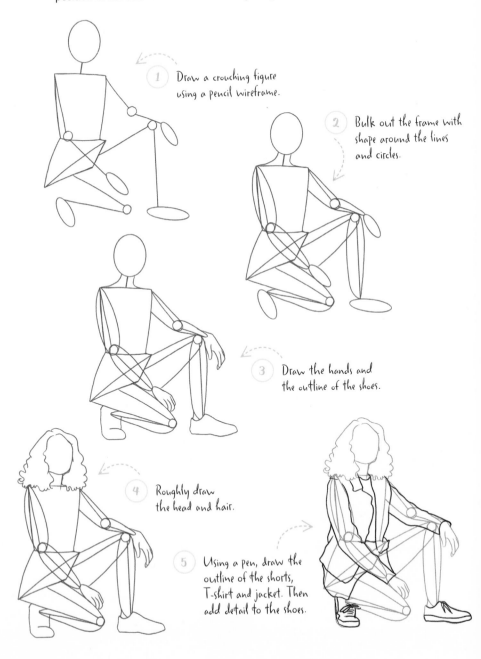

1. Draw a crouching figure using a pencil wireframe.

2. Bulk out the frame with shape around the lines and circles.

3. Draw the hands and the outline of the shoes.

4. Roughly draw the head and hair.

5. Using a pen, draw the outline of the shorts, T-shirt and jacket. Then add detail to the shoes.

6. Draw the outline of the hair in pen and add the facial features.

7. Trace the outline of the legs. Give the hair and clothing some detail.

8. Rub out the guidelines and add zips to the jacket and more strands to the hair.

9. Think about where the light is coming from and shade the darker areas.

10. Use a dark colour for the jacket but use a lighter colour where the light falls, to give the impression of leather.

Sitting girl

A relaxed sitting figure can seem daunting, but separating the body into simple shapes will help.

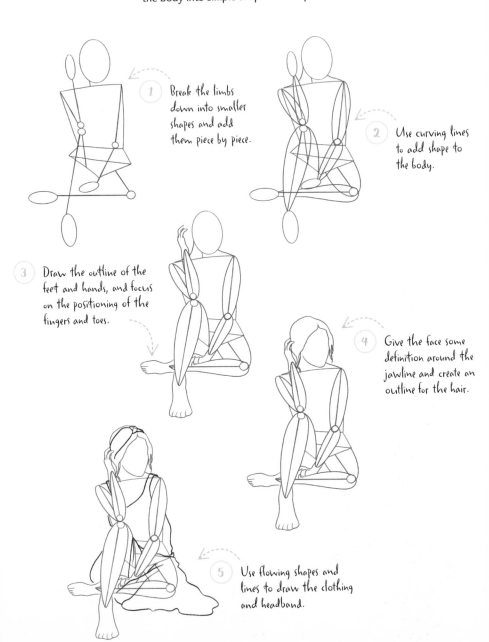

1 Break the limbs down into smaller shapes and add them piece by piece.

2 Use curving lines to add shape to the body.

3 Draw the outline of the feet and hands, and focus on the positioning of the fingers and toes.

4 Give the face some definition around the jawline and create an outline for the hair.

5 Use flowing shapes and lines to draw the clothing and headband.

6   Add basic facial features and an earring.

7   Trace the remaining body shape and give the toes nails. Add some shading around the neck and refine the face.

8   Rub out the wireframe, then use lines to show creases on the clothes.

9   Fill in the hair with a black pen and add shading along the lines of the body and to areas of clothing.

10   Start with the skin, then add colour to the clothing and use the colours in the patterned headband to tie the colours together.

Cool female pose

Creating an edgy look doesn't need to be difficult – draw a basic outline,
then add some shades and drape a jacket over her shoulders for a cool vibe.

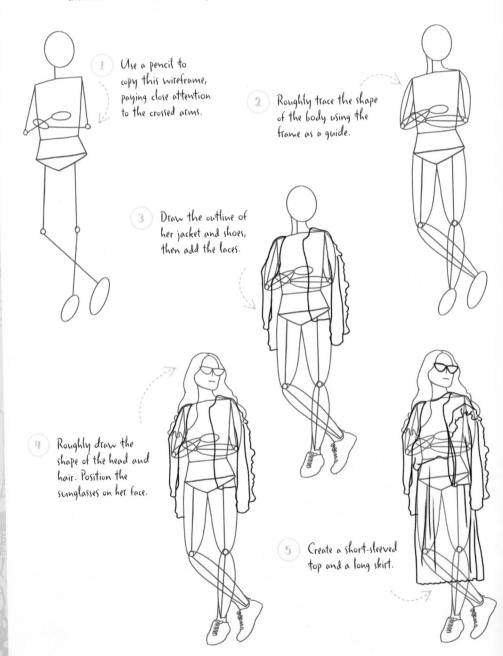

1. Use a pencil to copy this wireframe, paying close attention to the crossed arms.

2. Roughly trace the shape of the body using the frame as a guide.

3. Draw the outline of her jacket and shoes, then add the laces.

4. Roughly draw the shape of the head and hair. Position the sunglasses on her face.

5. Create a short-sleeved top and a long skirt.

6 Add facial features and give the hair more detail.

7 Where the arms and legs are visible, use the guides to draw them, then remove the guides.

8 Add detail to the face, hair and clothing.

9 Shade the dark areas.

10 Use dark colours for the shades and jacket but brighten the image up with a vivid colour for the skirt.

115

Easy standing boy

Take all the aspects you've learnt so far about the male body and put them together. Remember to give any visible muscles more definition.

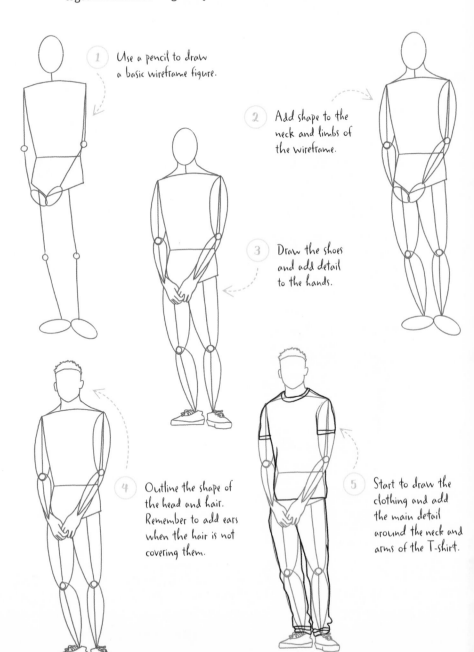

1   Use a pencil to draw a basic wireframe figure.

2   Add shape to the neck and limbs of the wireframe.

3   Draw the shoes and add detail to the hands.

4   Outline the shape of the head and hair. Remember to add ears when the hair is not covering them.

5   Start to draw the clothing and add the main detail around the neck and arms of the T-shirt.

6. Using the outline as a guide, create the hair. Next, draw the facial features and add detail to the ear. Use a pen to draw the rest of the body and shoes.

7. Add detail to the hair and add creases to the clothing.

8. Rub out the wireframe.

9. Shade the face, body and clothing.

10. Use a circular motion to add colour to the hair. Try adding patterns to the clothing using colour.

Male standing pose

Play with fun accessories and styling with this well-groomed man.

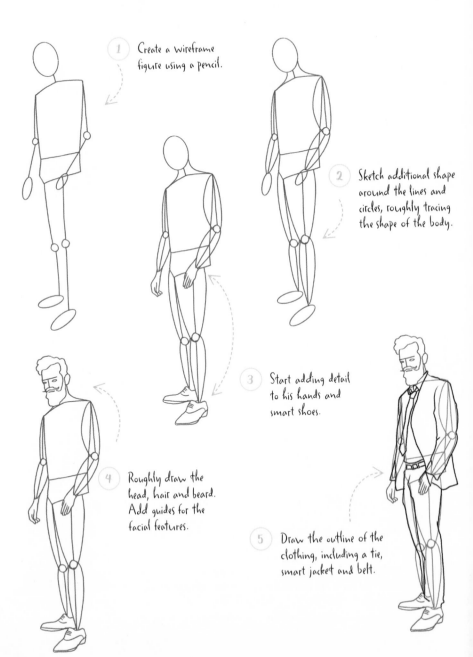

① Create a wireframe figure using a pencil.

② Sketch additional shape around the lines and circles, roughly tracing the shape of the body.

③ Start adding detail to his hands and smart shoes.

④ Roughly draw the head, hair and beard. Add guides for the facial features.

⑤ Draw the outline of the clothing, including a tie, smart jacket and belt.

6 Cover the eyes with sunglasses and start adding more detail to the face and hair. Complete the shoes.

7 Erase the guidelines.

8 Draw the individual strands of hair and add creases to the man's clothing.

9 Add shading, focusing on the clothing, hair and sunglasses.

10 Use a pinkish skin tone for the skin and a light brown for the hair. Use blue, red and orange for the clothing and accessories.

119

Skater boy

Give your drawing some added style by providing your character with some wheels. Once you've perfected this standing figure, try drawing him mid-jump.

1 Use a wireframe to position your man.

2 Give the figure shape around the lines and circles, tracing the shape of the body.

3 Draw the hands, then the shoes and skateboard.

4 Draw rough facial features and outline the hair and beard.

5 Give him tight trousers, a loose shirt and an open jacket.

6 Add detail to the face, shoes and skateboard.

7 Give the skateboard a striped design.

8 Rub out the guidelines.

9 Add shading, particularly on the clothing.

10 Give him a bright checked shirt for an indie vibe.

Male guitar player

Giving your character an object to hold and interact with can add movement and life to your drawing. Once you've perfected this man, try drawing the rest of his band.

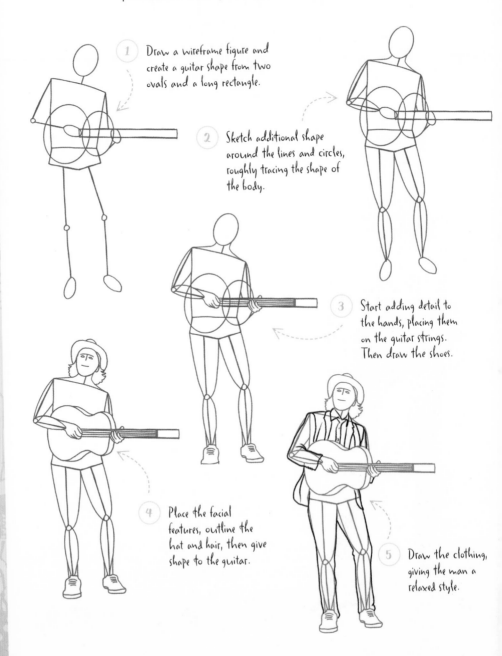

1 Draw a wireframe figure and create a guitar shape from two ovals and a long rectangle.

2 Sketch additional shape around the lines and circles, roughly tracing the shape of the body.

3 Start adding detail to the hands, placing them on the guitar strings. Then draw the shoes.

4 Place the facial features, outline the hat and hair, then give shape to the guitar.

5 Draw the clothing, giving the man a relaxed style.

6 Add detail to the face and hair. Finish the shoes.

7 Give the clothing some creases, detail and movement.

8 Finish the guitar and rub out the guides.

9 Shade the dark areas of your drawing.

10 Use a brown tone for the guitar and experiment with different colour choices for the clothing.

Perching man

This seated position is more relaxed and natural than a standing position, but can be drawn just as easily.

1. Using a pencil, create a wireframe figure perching on a wall.

2. Bulk out the body.

3. Draw the shoes, with detail for the laces.

4. Roughly draw the outline of the hair and the facial features.

5. Sketch the man's top, open jacket and turned-up jeans.

6 Add more detail to the facial features and the hair. Complete the shoes.

7 Rub out the guidelines.

8 Give his clothes more detail by adding creases.

9 Think about the darker areas and add shading.

10 Use black for the hair, a darker skin tone and cool colours for the clothing.

Leaning man

Start with a wireframe to capture this man. When you're done, why not fill in the rest of the scene? Is he leaning against a bar or a fence?

1. Use a pencil to draw a wireframe figure holding a newspaper.

2. Create the body shape by sketching additional shape around the lines and circles.

4. Roughly draw the head and the shape of the hair.

3. Start adding detail to the hands and the shoes.

5. Draw a suit and leave the top of the shirt beneath open for a casual look.

6 Add detail to the man's face and hair. Then add detail to his shoes.

7 Draw the newspaper and rub out the guidelines.

8 Give the fabric of his clothes and shoes more detail.

9 Add shading, focusing around the chin and on the jacket.

10 Add whichever skin tone you choose to the skin, then use a complementary tone for the hair. Keep the clothes monochrome.

About the artist

Justine Lecouffe is an artist, illustrator and graphic designer based in London, UK. She creates digital and traditional hand drawings encompassing fashion, beauty, architecture and travel, for clients in a wide range of industries, from book publishing to branding for jewellery and fashion designers.

Her work has been published in a number of books, including *Good Night Stories for Rebel Girls*, and her major clients include Apple, O2, National Trust, NHS, Redbull, Nivea and Pandora.

If you'd like to find out more information or to see further examples of her work find her on Instagram @justine_lcf

Acknowledgements

A million thanks to my cohabitation partner Gareth, who has been so supportive, cooking me dinner (or ordering me pizza) when I was drawing late at night!

And I'm immensely grateful to Abbie and the team at The Bright Press for such an amazing opportunity and the fantastic support they've given me throughout this project.